Dinosaurs

Caroline Clissold

Contents

Terrible Lizards	2
Walking Dinosaurs	4
Flying Reptiles	6
In the Sea	8
Food	10
Bones	12
Bone Diggers	14
Sum It Up	16

Terrible Lizards

Dinosaurs were very large reptiles. They lived a long time ago. *Dinosaur* means "terrible lizard."

FACT! There were more than 1,000 different kinds of dinosaur.

These dinosaurs are called *Tyrannosaurus rex*. If 3 more join them, how many will there be?

Some dinosaurs walked on 2 legs. Some walked on 4 legs. Count how many legs you see altogether.

KEY WORDS
- 1 more
- altogether
- count
- add

Some dinosaurs had horns. Some had spikes. Some had both. Add together the number of spikes and horns you can see here.

☐ spikes + ☐ horns = ☐ altogether

| 1 | 2 | 3 | 4 | 5 | 6 | 7 | 8 | 9 | 10 |

Walking Dinosaurs

This is a sauropod. Sauropods were the largest walking dinosaurs. They had long necks and long tails.

Each foot has 5 toes. How many toes are there on 2 feet?

KEY WORDS

- add
- how many?
- total
- altogether

Prosauropods walked on 2 legs, but they had small front legs.

Look at the prosauropod footprints. Add them together. How many are there in total?

Including the front legs, how many legs would 3 prosauropods have altogether?

1 2 3 4 5 6 7 8 9 10 11 12

Flying Reptiles

This is a pterosaur. It had skin between its arms and body. This worked like wings for flying.

Here are different kinds of pterosaurs. Count the total number of wings. Write it down.

KEY WORDS
- altogether
- total
- add
- count

Pterodactyls were a kind of pterosaur. They ate fish. Look at the table. Which pterodactyl ate the most? Add the number of fish they ate altogether.

Pterodactyl	Number of fish
A	3
B	4
C	1
D	2

How many more fish did A eat than C?

TOOLS

| 1 | 2 | 3 | 4 | 5 | 6 | 7 | 8 | 9 | 10 |

In the Sea

These are ichthyosaurs. They looked like dolphins. They had flippers, fins, and long beaks. Count all the flippers and fins you can see on 1 ichthyosaur.

Sea crocodiles lived with the dinosaurs. Today, most crocodiles live in rivers and lakes. How many are there in total?

This ichthyosaur is fighting another dinosaur that swims – a plesiosaur. If 2 more plesiosaurs joined them, how many would there be?

KEY WORDS
- total
- count all
- how many more?
- plus

Pliosaurs had much bigger mouths than plesiosaurs. Kronosaurus was the largest pliosaur. It ate sharks. How many more sharks are there than pliosaurs?

1 2 3 4 5 6 7 8 9 10

Food

There were 2 groups of dinosaur. One kind only ate plants. The other kind ate mostly meat.

Brontosaurs ate plants.

These are triceratops. They were plant-eaters. How many horns does each have? How many are there altogether?

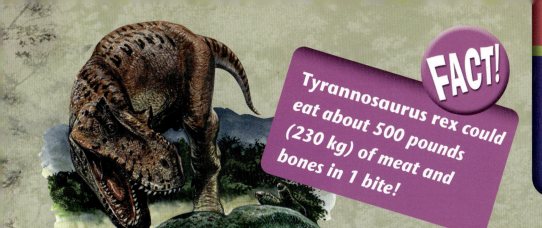

KEY WORDS
- altogether
- total
- how many?
- groups

FACT! Tyrannosaurus rex could eat about 500 pounds (230 kg) of meat and bones in 1 bite!

Tyrannosaurus rex ate meat. If it ate 1 dinosaur every day, how many would it eat in 6 days?

The Brachiosaurus ate groups of plants. Which groups could it eat to make a total of 10 plants?

Groups of plants	Number
Ferns	3
Cycads	4
Pine trees	2
Leaves	6
Fruit	5

TOOLS

Bones

- This is a thigh bone from an Antarctosaurus compared to a man. Which is taller?

- This is the actual size of a dinosaur's skull. How long is it?

KEY WORDS
- taller
- compare
- how long?

This is the skeleton of a dinosaur. How tall is it in this picture?

How many bones are in 1 leg?
How many are in all 4 legs?

TOOLS

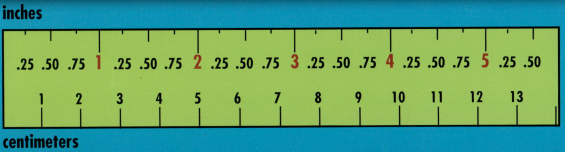

Bone Diggers

These people are called paleontologists. They dig for fossils. Fossils are very old dinosaur bones or prints in earth or rocks. How many people can you count?

This is a fossil of a dinosaur. Estimate how many ribs there are.

KEY WORDS

- how many?
- estimate
- group
- count

Richard Owen was the first dinosaur expert. He found lots of fossils. He was the first person to use the word *dinosaur*.

Look at these groups of dinosaur bones. How many of each kind can you count?

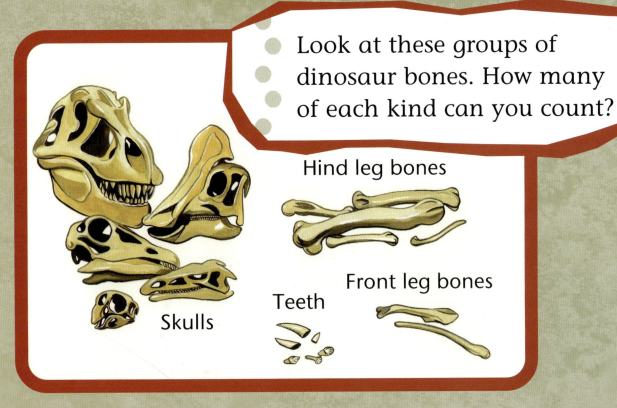

Hind leg bones

Front leg bones

Teeth

Skulls

TOOLS

| 1 | 2 | 3 | 4 | 5 | 6 | 7 | 8 | 9 | 10 |
| 11 | 12 | 13 | 14 | 15 | 16 | 17 | 18 | 19 | 20 |

Sum It Up

Here are 2 groups of dinosaurs.
There are meat-eaters and plant-eaters.
Write a formula to show how many there are altogether.
Use **+** and **=** in your formula.

Are there more meat-eaters or plant-eaters? How can you tell?